This book belongs to:

_____

_____

Thank you from Caroline Milmine, Author

My six wonderful children, family and of course, my cat, Pickle, thank you for believing in me and for all your support.

Gregor for everything you do.

Andrew L. Ramirez for your invaluable guidance.

Anna Bondarenko – thank you so much for bringing this Basey Bear story to life. You have worked incredibly hard and I am so grateful for your illustrating talent, patience and friendship throughout this project.

Heidi Cook, my fabulous editor. I rely on your wise advice!

Harriet Bishop – for her fantastic design skills! You are the best!

Roy Haylock & Elliott Smith, who both inspire me creatively.

With special mention to all my friends and colleagues. Thank you for your support over the years, with special mention to Audrey and Julia.

For Christine - always and forever, my best friend. Thank you so much for your support, love and encouragement over so many years.

Thank you from Anna Bondarenko, Illustrator

I want to express my gratitude to my whole family - my beloved husband Eduard, two wonderful daughters Olivia and Nicole, dear mother Irina and father Igor, who always admire and support my work. To my illustrator friends who inspire me, with whom we share professional experience and help each other grow. I would like to express my gratitude to all creative people for bringing new, beautiful, interesting things into the world, for giving themselves to their favorite work entirely, for giving us magical energy and a piece of their soul along with their works.

Design: Harriet Bishop
Illustration: Anna Bondarenko
Copyright © 2023
Caroline Milmine

ISBN: 978-1-7384098-0-8

Basey Bear
Got Angry!

Caroline Milmine

Illustrated by Anna Bondarenko

Basey Bear did care about others, but sometimes,
he lost his temper and took his anger out on everyone around him.
For example, Basey got angry the time his little sister,
Bizzi, broke his favourite toy.

Basey Bear also got angry on the playground at school.

"Basey Bear, we don't want to play football,"
said his friends. "We're playing a skipping game, instead."

Basey Bear wasn't happy about the skipping game,
but he didn't want to play on his own.
All was going well until Basey felt the rope tighten on one side.

Then,
he fell over.

Their teacher, Mrs. Bearton, took Basey aside.
"You shouldn't hurt your friends, Basey. We need to use our words to solve our problems. You hurt Bobby, and you need to apologise to him," Mrs. Bearton told Basey. Basey refused to say sorry,

By the time Mrs. Bearton had dealt with Basey's poor behaviour, there was no break time left.

But... could he help it?

No!

Because Basey Bear got angry!

On Saturday, Basey and Bizzi Bear were enjoying
a family day out at the zoo with their Mum and Dad.
"I can't wait to see the monkeys, Bizzi! What do you
want to see?" Basey said. "I like elephants," Bizzi replied.

To get into the zoo, Basey and his family had
to pass through the zoo gift shop.

Suddenly, he spotted an amazing,
fluffy monkey toy. It looked
just like a real monkey!

"Mum, Dad, please buy it for me,"
begged Basey Bear.

"No, Basey," said Dad, "You've been unkind at home and at school this week."

"Please, Dad!" pleaded Basey Bear. "No," said Dad firmly.

Basey Bear threw himself onto the floor of the shop.

Mum, Dad, and Bizzi were very upset that Basey had ruined their special day out to the zoo.

In the end, Dad had to call Grandma to come and take Basey home with her while the rest of the family finished their zoo trip.

As a result of Basey Bear's behaviour, he did not get the monkey toy he wanted. He also missed out on seeing the rest of the animals at the zoo.

But... could he help it?

No!

Because Basey Bear got angry!

"You've upset your friends and family
by getting so angry," said Grandma.

Basey Bear felt sad. He realised he had to change his behaviour.
"I want to stay calm, Grandma, but I don't know how," said Basey.

"Don't worry, Basey," said Grandma, kindly. "We will all help you."

Grandma talked to Basey's Mum and Dad about what he had told her.

Then, Basey Bear's parents talked to his teacher.

The next day, Mrs. Bearton asked her class what they did to help them stay calm when they got angry.

$$\frac{1}{2} + \frac{1}{2} = 1$$

Is it a half?

Maths

"My parents tell me to take some deep breaths in and out until I feel calmer," said Ben Bear.

"Counting to 10 over and over is what helps me," explained Bo Bear.

"A big hug calms me down,"
smiled Bella Bear.

."I like to sit somewhere quiet
and colour, or read a book,"
said Bobby Bear.

"I like to run fast on the spot
until I feel too tired to be angry,"
said Bonnie Bear.

"These are some
great ideas, class!"
said Mrs Bearton.

"You could also find a
quiet corner and sit there,
or try having a drink of water.
Listening to music might
also help us to calm down.

And, after we've calmed down, we should
always apologise if we hurt someone.

Saying 'sorry' is the right thing to do,
and it will always make you both feel better,"
explained Basey's teacher.

Basey was very surprised that the other children had problems with their anger, too.

Basey Bear decided he needed to say 'sorry' to his friends and family.
His teacher was right! Everyone did feel better.

From that day on, Basey Bear tried hard to change
his ways and make things right again.

From then on, Basey Bear tried hard to stay calm and not lose his temper.

For example, when Bizzi wasn't playing carefully with his toys, Basey would take some deep breaths in and out to calm himself down.

Basey learned that counting to ten really helped when he got frustrated with his friends at school. When he did his counting, he had more fun at playtime, even when they didn't play the games he suggested.

Basey Bear is much happier now,
and so are his family and friends.

Why?
Because Basey Bear
discovered...
He could change
his ways and,

Yes!

He could control his anger!

About the Author

Caroline Milmine finds great happiness in writing. In addition to children's books, she has written short stories and poems. She even has a film script and a series of historical novels in the works!

Caroline holds an MA (Hons) in Sociology from Glasgow University, a Postgraduate Certification in Education from Strathclyde University in Glasgow, and a Postgraduate Certification in Information Systems Management from De Montfort University in Milton Keynes. She currently works as a Teaching Assistant at a primary school. Caroline teaches RWI and Fresh Start Phonics. She also provides support for children to succeed at school through help in the classroom and in her intervention groups.

In her free time, she likes reading, especially classic authors. Caroline also likes watching classic movies and not so classic funny videos!

Caroline wants to help children develop a love for reading and to encourage all children to be kind, thoughtful and inclusive towards others. To these ends, Caroline will continue doing what she loves the most: writing children's books, mainly ones featuring naughty animals who learn valuable lessons.

You can find Caroline Milmine, and information about all of her new books, in the following places:

caroline.milmine.uk
facebook.com/Caroline.Milmine.Author
instagram.com/carolinemilmine/

Anna Bondarenko has been drawing since childhood. At school, she designed and drew all kinds of posters. People told her mother that Anna should be sent to art school. At art school, a very talented teacher quickly helped Anna progress in her drawings and assisted her entrance into the Faculty of Architecture. After graduation, Anna worked for three years in the field of 3D visualization. The technical knowledge and techniques involved in architecture and 3D programmes greatly contributed to Anna's skills as a children's book illustrator.

In her free time, Anna likes to travel, read, paint, and spend time with her family. In addition to drawing, Anna enjoys sewing and knitting and the satisfaction of making something to hold in her own hands.

Note from the Illustrator:
The book "Basey Bear Got Angry" differs from the previous books in the variety of characters illustrated. I showed scenes with many bears and Basey's school mates. Everyone has different emotions and moods. Some are sitting, others are running and some are jumping rope. It's not easy to single out one illustration that I enjoyed drawing the most. It was interesting to draw zoos scenes and show Basey's changeable mood. This little bear has experienced everything from joy to disappointment!
Sincerely, Anna Bondarenko

You can learn more about Anna in the following places:

instagram.com/hanna_boanna/
facebook.com/anna.gaydabas/
email.boanna@gmail.com

You can follow Basey Bear on Facebook!
facebook.com/baseybear

If you enjoy *Basey Bear Got Angry*, will you consider
writing an honest review of my book on Amazon?
For a self-publishing author, reviews are incredibly
important to the success of any new book.

Thank you very much for your time
- Caroline Milmine.

Other books available in the Basey Bear series:

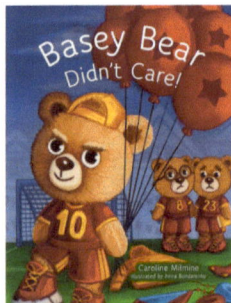

www.ingramcontent.com/pod-product-compliance
Lightning Source LLC
Chambersburg PA
CBHW042124040426

42450CB00002B/64